A VISION OF INDIA

NOBEL LAUREATES

With Love
to dear Tara
Visit to India
in Millennium 2000!
from
Rangappa Pata
July 14th Friday, 2000.

Written by
Swarn Khandpur

Visualised & Illustrated by
D. Y. Acharekar

NAVNEET PUBLICATIONS (INDIA) LIMITED

CONTENTS

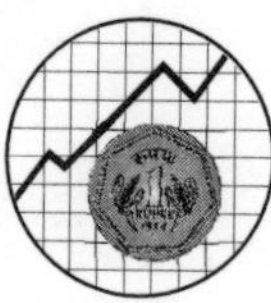

Published by
Navneet Publications (India) Ltd.,
Bhavani Shankar Road, Dadar,
Mumbai – 400 028. India
Tel. 430 7286 Fax: 437 2568
Visit us at: www.navneet.com
e-mail: navneet1@.vsnl.com

Offices:
• **Ahmedabad**
Navneet House, Gurukul Road, Memnagar,
Ahmedabad – 380 052. Tel. 745 1000 / 741 1110
• **Pune**
Sita Park, 18, Shivaji Nagar,
Near Bharat English School,
Pune – 411 005. Tel. 553 6364
• **Nagpur**
Agge Apartments,
Agyaramdevi –S.T. Stand Road,
Nagpur – 440 018. Tel. 724411
• **Chennai**
30, Sriram Nagar, North Street, Alwarpet,
Chennai – 600 018. Tel. 434 6404

Printed at : Printmann, Mumbai – 400 013

ISBN 81-243-0400-9

Price : Rs.

99 (2)

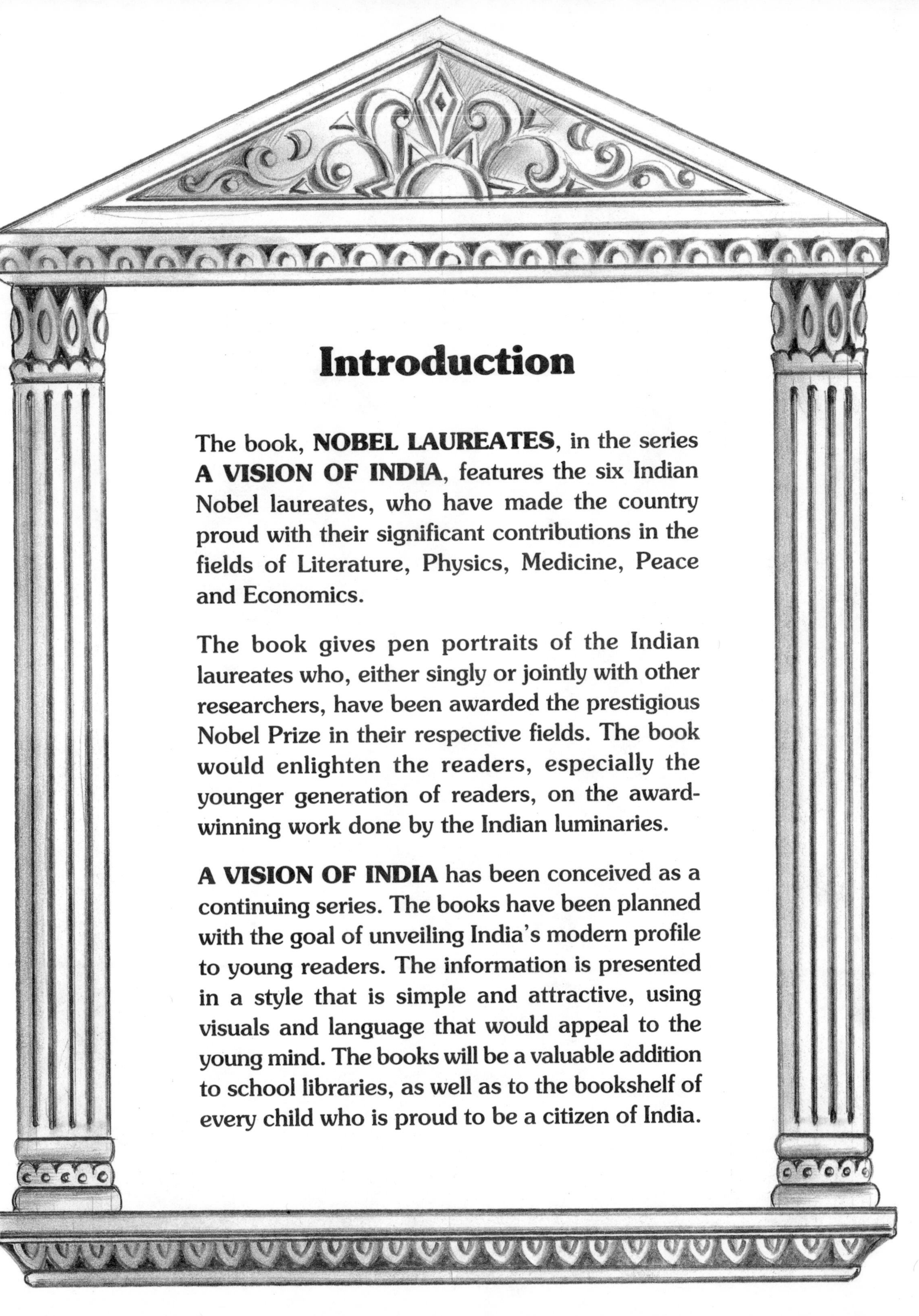

Introduction

The book, **NOBEL LAUREATES**, in the series **A VISION OF INDIA**, features the six Indian Nobel laureates, who have made the country proud with their significant contributions in the fields of Literature, Physics, Medicine, Peace and Economics.

The book gives pen portraits of the Indian laureates who, either singly or jointly with other researchers, have been awarded the prestigious Nobel Prize in their respective fields. The book would enlighten the readers, especially the younger generation of readers, on the award-winning work done by the Indian luminaries.

A VISION OF INDIA has been conceived as a continuing series. The books have been planned with the goal of unveiling India's modern profile to young readers. The information is presented in a style that is simple and attractive, using visuals and language that would appeal to the young mind. The books will be a valuable addition to school libraries, as well as to the bookshelf of every child who is proud to be a citizen of India.

Alfred Bernhard Nobel

(1833 - 1896)

Alfred Bernhard Nobel, who instituted the Nobel Prizes, was born in Stockholm (Sweden) in 1833. His father was an expert in explosives. Alfred was never formally educated, but he had a talent for invention and was a competent chemist at the age of sixteen. After studying chemistry in France and the United States, he went into the family business of making explosives and set up a small factory near Stockholm in Sweden. A few incidents of blasts in his factory led him to be called a 'mad scientist'.

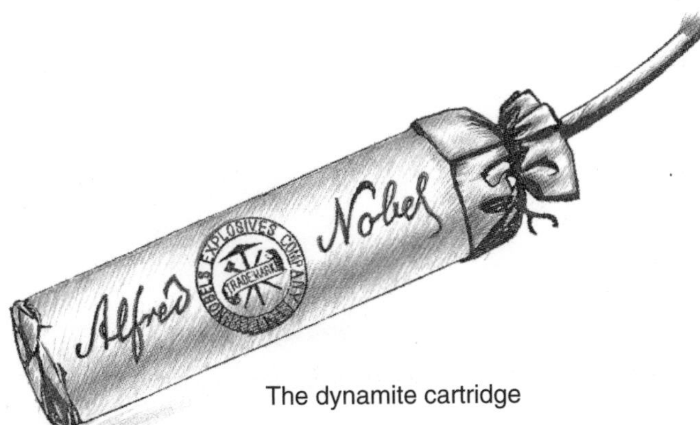

The dynamite cartridge

At that time, nitroglycerine was used as an explosive. It was a very powerful and extremely dangerous explosive. Alfred tried many ways of developing its safer form. By adding a fine, porous powder called *kieselguhr*, he invented a safe, easily handled explosive. Alfred named the new explosive 'dynamite'. He received a patent for it in 1867. Construction companies, mining companies and the governments of various countries, ordered large quantities of dynamite because of its relative safety and explosive power. He went on to develop other new explosives. Alfred set up factories around the world, which produced a vast range of explosives. The sales of dynamite and other explosives brought him great wealth. He became a millionaire.

It so happened that when his elder brother died of heart trouble, a leading French newspaper misread the report and ran an obituary of Alfred Nobel, calling him 'a merchant of death'. Upon seeing the obituary, Nobel was stunned. He realised the potential misuse of his invention. The feeling of guilt led him to do something 'noble' for the world. So before he died, he left in his will, a fund of about nine million dollars, the interest of which was to provide five annual awards as Nobel Prizes, to those who did the most to advance the cause of peace, literature and the sciences.

The Nobel Prizes, first awarded in the year 1901, remain the most honoured prizes in the world.

The obverse side of the Nobel medal
In Latin: Alfred Nobel,
Birth: 1833, Death: 1896

The Medal for Physiology or Medicine

The Medal for Peace

The Medal for Physics and Chemistry

The Medal for Literature

The Medal for Economic Sciences

The Nobel Prize

The Nobel Prize is considered the most prestigious prize in the world. It is awarded annually to people or institutions for outstanding contributions in a variety of fields for the good of humanity.

The prize is named after Alfred Nobel, who in his will directed that the interest from the funds be set aside and used to give one annual prize in each of the five fields of **Physics, Chemistry, Physiology or Medicine** and **Literature** and the 'most effective work in the interest of international **Peace**'. The prizes were first presented in 1901. A sixth prize — the Nobel Memorial Prize in **Economic Sciences** — was instituted in 1968, by the National Bank of Sweden, and was first awarded in 1969.

These six Nobel Prizes are awarded every year on December 10, the death anniversary of Alfred Nobel. Each recipient is presented a gold medal, a certificate bearing the awardee's name and field of achievement, and a cash prize. The obverse side of each medal has a bust of Alfred Nobel. The reverse side of each of the medals, other than those for Physics and Chemistry, which have identical reverse sides, is different. The prize-giving ceremony is held in Stockholm, Sweden. The Peace Prize, however, is awarded in Oslo, Norway.

The prize-winners are chosen by different committees whose members are selected by the Swedish Academies and Institute and the Norwegian parliament. The candidates are chosen from among the names recommended by eminent scholars, former Nobel Prize winners and distinguished scientists. The candidate does not apply for the prize directly. Sometimes two or three winners share the prize and sometimes no candidate is found suitable for a particular prize in that year.

In his will, Alfred Nobel had mentioned: "...It is my express wish that in awarding the prizes no consideration whatever shall be given to the nationality of the candidates, but that the most worthy shall receive the prize, whether he be a Scandinavian or not."

EUROPE
NORWAY
SWEDEN
FINLAND
OSLO
STOCKHOLM
ESTONIA
RUSSIA
LATVIA
LITHUANIA
UNITED KINGDOM
BELARUS
POLAND
GERMANY
CZECH REP.
UKRAINE
FRANCE
SLOVAKIA
SWITZERLAND
AUSTRIA
HUNGARY
ROMANIA
ITALY

The Bard of Santiniketan

Rabindranath Tagore

(1861 - 1941)

Where the mind is without fear and
the head is held high;
Where knowledge is free;
Where the world has not been broken up
into fragments by narrow domestic walls;
Where words come out from the
depth of truth;
Where tireless striving stretches its
arms towards perfection;
Where the clear stream of reason has
not lost its way into the dreary desert
sand of dead habit;
Where the mind is led forward by
Thee into ever-widening thought and action —
Into that heaven of freedom, my
Father, let my country awake.

This is one of the poems in the English version of the original Bengali *Gitanjali* (Song Offerings) for which Rabindranath Tagore was awarded the Nobel Prize for Literature in 1913.

Rabindranath Tagore, fondly called 'Gurudev', is one of the great sons of India. He was a genius in many ways. A lover of nature, Tagore wrote not only poetry, but plays, dance-dramas, stories, novels and numerous songs as well. Besides, he was a great educationist. It is difficult to find another equally versatile and gifted genius in history.

The Tagores were hereditary landowners (*zamindars*) of Bengal. Originally called Banerjis, they came to be known as 'Thakurs' (respected lord) because of their aristocratic way of life. The name was later anglicised to 'Tagore'.

Rabindranath was born on May 6, 1861, in the rambling old mansion of the Tagore family at Jorasanko, Calcutta. Being the fourteenth child of his parents, young

The Medal for Literature (reverse side)
[The inscription reads (word for word): Inventions enhance life which is beautified through art]

Open-air classes at Tagore's Santiniketan

Rabindra grew up under the care of the family's servants.

From the very beginning, young Rabindra would not conform to the teaching of a conventional school or to learning at home under the care of tutors. Schools were like prison to him, where, "we had to sit inert, like dead specimens of some museum, while lessons were pelted at us like hailstones on flowers."

The first nursery rhyme, a common jingle in Bengali which he had learnt, revealed to him the magic of poetry. He wrote his first verse when he was only seven. From then on, whenever he found time, he would sit down with a notebook and write poems. What he wrote was so beautiful that well-known writers of the day were full of admiration for him. One of them, the doyen of Bengali literature, Bankim Chandra Chatterji, once took off a garland from his neck and put it on young Rabindra, saying that it was more fitting to garland the 'rising sun'.

Having suffered from bad teaching in his childhood, Tagore thought of starting a small experimental school, modelled on the ancient ideals of the Gurukula. He had liked Santiniketan (Abode of Peace), a place 150 km from Calcutta, when he had visited it earlier with his father.

So on December 22, 1901, Tagore began his school at Santiniketan, with five pupils. He named it *Brahmacharya Ashram*, after the ancient forest hermitages. He wanted to provide children an environment where the mind of the young "might expand into love of Beauty and of God". He did not like to impose on children the conventional school system which he himself had hated.

The best teacher, according to Tagore was nature. The classes in his school were therefore held in the open, under the trees, and students were encouraged to observe and love nature in its changing moods. "No less important," said Tagore, "is the influence of music and of the fine arts in training the child's emotions and his sensibility." He instituted a number of seasonal festivals so that the students might

grow in communion with Nature, learn to enjoy her bounties and develop their aesthetic sense.

Tagore himself would supervise the routine of the school and participate in all its activities. He taught the children himself. When he found that there were no suitable primers and textbooks available in Bengali, he wrote them himself.

It was while Tagore was in Santiniketan that the news came of his getting the Nobel Prize for his *Gitanjali*, a collection of 103 poems. The children, who hardly knew what the Nobel Prize was, understood that their beloved Gurudev had been honoured by the world, and went wild with joy. Tagore himself felt elated and proud that his country's name had been put on the world's literary map and that he was the reason for it.

Gitanjali was translated from the original Bengali into English by Tagore himself. W.B. Yeats, the famous Irish poet, wrote the introduction for *Gitanjali*. He felt that, "the entire western world had been waiting for a poet like him [Tagore]".

Tagore's experiment at Santiniketan proved to be a great success. He thought of widening the scope of studies of the school to a university. He thought of an international university where scholars from all over the world would come together, each teaching and learning something from the other. He was seeking to develop a base on which the cultures of the East and the West could meet in fellowship and strengthen the conditions for world peace. He named the university 'Visva-Bharati', and selected as its motto, a Sanskrit verse meaning: 'Where the world makes its home in a single nest'. He built another institution, Sriniketan, to work for village uplift.

A lover of forests, Tagore was against the ruthless deforestation of the country side. He thought of introducing a practice which would catch the popular imagination and make people plant trees for the love of them. He introduced two seasonal festivals *Vriksharopana* (Tree-planting) and *Hala-karshana* (Ploughing) at Santiniketan and Sriniketan during the rainy season. The picturesque festivals, with simple ceremonies accompanied by music and dance, invoking nature's fertility, are still celebrated annually and attract visitors.

The tree-planting ceremony initiated by Tagore is now an all-India festival actively sponsored by the Central and State governments.

Tagore had a keen interest in the folk music of Bengal. "One day I chanced to hear a Baul [a wandering musician of Bengal] strumming an *ektara*, singing of a universal God. Since then I have often sought to understand these people whose songs are their only form of worship. I have fitted the tunes of the Bauls to many of my songs." A good singer himself, Tagore composed more than a thousand songs. Collectively known as 'Rabindra Sangeet', these songs are in a class by themselves. They are very popular in Bengal and are sung by one and all. One of his songs, *Jana gana mana*, is the national anthem of India. Another of his songs, *Amar Sonar Bangla* (My Golden Bengal), is the national anthem of Bangladesh.

Tagore's creative genius was many-sided. He took to painting quite late in life. Although he did not use the brush, he doodled freely with his pen. His manuscripts bear ample and fascinating evidence of these playful exercises which are interwoven with his verses.

Two great souls — Gandhiji and Tagore at Santiniketan

The ghastly massacre of Jallianwala Bagh at Amritsar on April 13, 1919, deeply perturbed Tagore. He wrote a letter to the Viceroy, stating that the brutality of the action was 'without parallel in the history of civilised Government...' He renounced the knighthood, with its title 'Sir', which the British Government had bestowed on him, in protest against the inhuman killings.

The two 'makers' of modern India Gandhiji and Tagore, were drawn to each other. It was perhaps Tagore's love for his country that brought him closer to Gandhiji. He acknowledged Gandhiji's greatness by calling him 'Mahatma', the Great Soul, and 'as one belonging to all humanity'.

Although radically different in their idealism, Tagore and the Mahatma had a special kind of bond throughout their lives. Gandhiji had visited Santiniketan several times. Once, he told the inmates of the ashram that they must do wholly without hired labour and take upon themselves the responsibilities of keeping the ashram clean, and of running all its services, including the cooking of food, washing of dishes, etc. The pupils and teachers warmly welcomed Gandhiji's advice. The experiment was launched but it did not last very long. Yet, every year, March 10 is observed as Gandhi Day and all the paid help are given a holiday. The teachers and pupils do all the cooking themselves and give a spring-cleaning to the *ashram* on this day.

Rabindranath breathed his last on August 7, 1941, in the same old Jorasanko house where he had first opened his eyes 80 years and three months earlier. It was the day of the full moon of *Sravana*, the month of rains, so often celebrated in his poems and songs.

Tagore had earlier written a song in Bengali which he had desired should be sung at his death. It was:

In front lies the ocean of peace,
launch the boat, Helmsman,
you will be the comrade ever...

The song is still sung at each death anniversary of India's great poet.

DO YOU KNOW ?

- The *Vedas* are the oldest Sanskrit literature. More than 3,000 years old, they contain hymns composed in praise of every element and force of Nature. Four in number, they are the *Rig Veda*, the *Yajur Veda*, the *Sam Veda* and the *Atharva Veda*.
- The *Mahabharata*, with one lakh verses, is considered the longest poem in the world. The sage-poet Vedavyasa, the author of the *Mahabharata*, is said to have had the service of Lord Ganesha as his scribe!
- The *Bhagvad Gita*, 'the Song of the Lord', although a part of the *Mahabharata*, is a complete book in itself. It is a poem of seven hundred verses, written in the form of a dialogue. The *Gita* was first translated into English by Charles Wilkingson in 1785. It has been translated into about 60 languages of the world.
- *Adi Granth,* the holy book of the Sikhs, has a major portion of its verses set to music (in different classical *raagas*) and is thus sung.
- Kalidasa is acknowledged as the greatest poet and dramatist of Sanskrit literature. When the English translation of his drama *Abhijnyan Shakuntalam* appeared in Europe, it created a sensation of sorts among the intellectuals. From Sir William Jones's English translation, the *Shakuntalam* appeared in German, French, Danish and Italian.
- The animal fables of the *Jatakas*, which recount the previous births of the Buddha, inspired many other animal and folk stories of Europe and Western Asia.
- *Panchatantra* (A Collection of Five Books) is the oldest collection of fables in Sanskrit. Among its two hundred versions, are the famous *Aesop's Fables* which were also based on the *Panchatantra* stories.
- Some of the English language's most familiar sayings and words come from the holy book of the Christians, the *Bible* — from the *Old Testament* in particular, for instance, '*Pride goeth* before destruction' and 'an haughty spirit *before a fall*' (Proverbs 16, Verse 18).

The Celebrated Genius

Dr. C. V. Raman

(1888 - 1970)

During a long sea voyage to Europe in 1921 as a representative of the Calcutta University at a science meet, C.V. Raman, the young physicist, wondered why the water in the Mediterranean Sea was such a dark shade of blue. The answer to this apparently simple question, which he finally unravelled, won him the world's most prestigious award — the Nobel Prize.

Dr. Chandrasekhara Venkata Raman was possibly the greatest physicist this country has ever produced. His pioneering research on the molecular scattering of light, the phenomenon that causes changes in the nature of light when it passes through a transparent medium — solid, liquid or gaseous — culminated in his getting the Nobel Prize for Physics in 1930. Raman's interest in physical optics appeared to have derived, in large measures, from his fascination with the aesthetics of colour. He conducted a series of experiments on the sun rays passing through water, transparent ice blocks and other media. For these experiments, Raman used a mercury arc and a spectograph. He obtained some new lines in the spectrum on passing the sun rays through different substances. These lines were later called 'Raman Lines' and the discovery, the 'Raman Effect'.

Born in an orthodox South Indian Brahmin family in 1888 at Thiruvanaikkaval near Tiruchirapalli, Tamil Nadu, Raman proved to be a brilliant student. He passed his matriculation at the age of 11, and at 15 graduated from the Presidency College, Madras. Raman wanted to go abroad after his graduation, but a British doctor disqualified him on medical grounds, saying that he would not be able to withstand the rigours of the English climate. After completing his

The Medal for Physics (reverse side)
[The inscription reads (word for word): Inventions enhance life which is beautified through art]

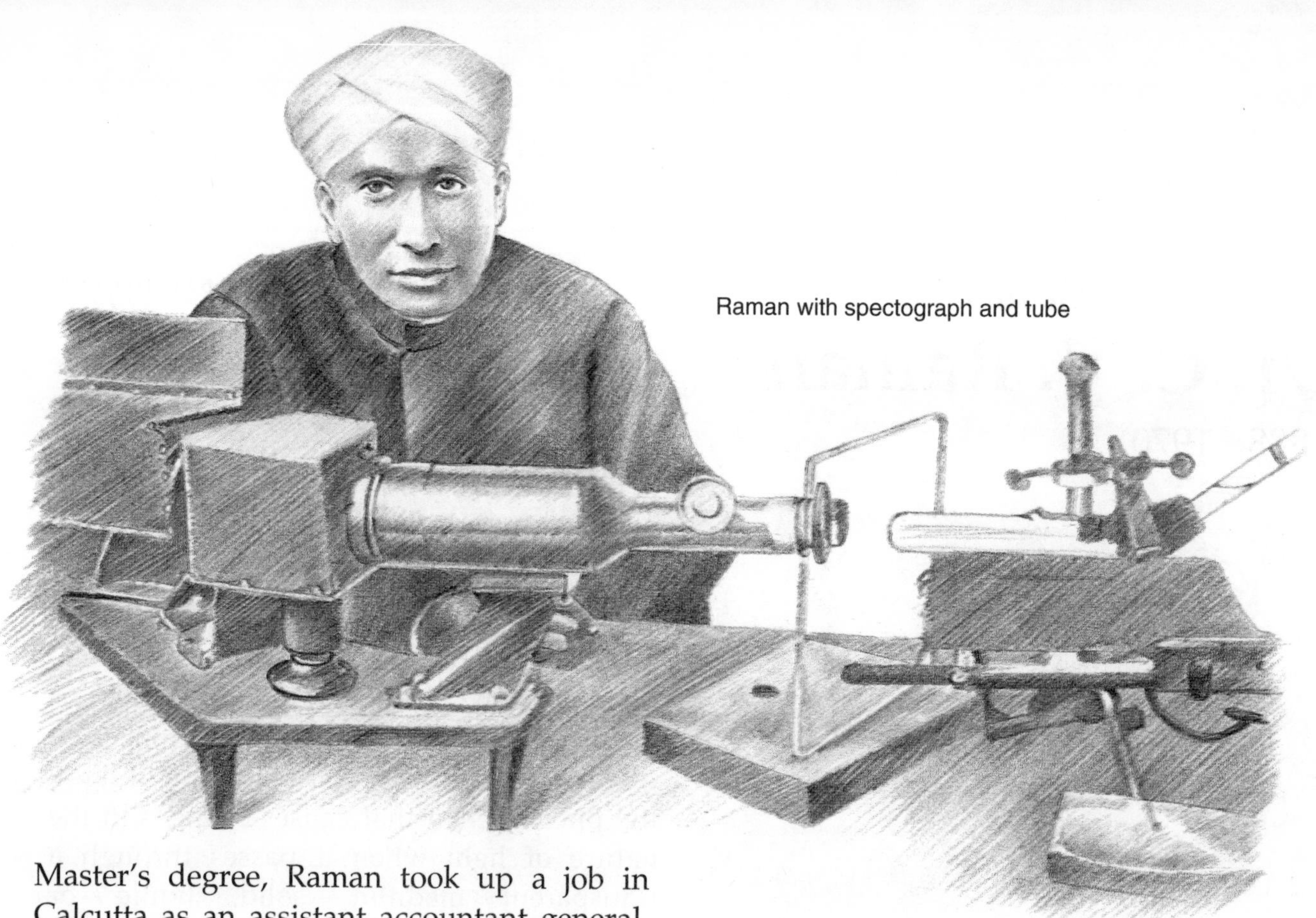

Raman with spectograph and tube

Master's degree, Raman took up a job in Calcutta as an assistant accountant general. But his interest in science did not decrease. He would spend most of his spare time in the mornings and evenings in the laboratory of the Indian Association for Cultivation of Science.

After ten years of government service, Raman resigned to work as a professor of physics at the Calcutta University, despite the fact that the University paid him a lower salary than the government did. It was at the University laboratory that Raman did the most important research of his life.

The world was not slow to recognise the importance of C.V. Raman's achievements. "When the Nobel award was announced, I saw it as a personal triumph, an achievement, a recognition for a very remarkable discovery, for reaching the goal I had pursued for seven years. But when I sat in that crowded hall and I saw the sea of western faces surrounding me, and I, the only Indian, in my turban and closed coat, it dawned on me that I was really representing my people and my country. I felt truly humble when I received the prize from King Gustav; it was a moment of great emotion, but I could restrain myself. Then I turned round and saw the British Union Jack under which I had been sitting and it was then that I realized that my poor country, India, did not even have a flag of her own — and it was this that triggered off my complete breakdown." He was so moved by emotions that tears started streaming down his face.

Raman was proud to be an Indian. Till the day he died, he did not give up his traditional Indian turban in favour of a European hat. In those days, going abroad was a rare event, and people were always curious to learn about one's foreign experiences. "Did you not find it embarrassing to move around London in a turban?" Raman was asked.

"Young man," he replied, "I will tell you about a little incident that happened while I was in London. One evening I went to the Royal Institution to hear a lecture by Lord Rutherford. I arrived a little late and by that

time the lecture had started. And so I quietly slipped into one of the back rows and sat there. Suddenly, Lord Rutherford looked at me and said, 'Professor Raman, why are you sitting there all alone in the back row? Come up here to the front.' I then went and sat in the front row with all the famous British scientists. After the lecture, I asked Rutherford, 'Professor, how did you recognise me? This is my first trip to England and we have never met so far.' Rutherford replied, 'Well, I have read your papers and when I saw a person in the audience wearing a Madrasi turban, I knew it must be you.' So young man, now you tell me what is wrong with a Madrasi turban?''

In 1933, Raman left his professorship in Calcutta for the Indian Institute of Science in Bangalore. There he served as its director until 1937 and as head of the physics department until 1948.

Raman was instrumental in establishing the Indian Academy of Sciences in 1934, to encourage talented scientists in their research. He pioneered scientific journals on the lines of the journals published by the Royal Society, London. The dozen or so journals published by the Academy today, trace their origins to Raman's times. "Do not allow the Academy's journals to die — for they are sensitive indicators of the quality of science done in the country. They will tell us whether science is really taking root in the country or not,'' he used to say. He would arrange popular lectures in schools and colleges to persuade the youth to devote themselves to science. His ability to talk on scientific subjects in simple language was such that at least a handful of India's scientists today state that they took to science because of Raman.

One of his ambitions was to secure a prominent place for India on the scientific map of the world. He wanted opportunities to be created in the country for scientists, so that they need not look outside for inspiration. "The essence of science," he said, "is independent thinking and hard work, not equipment."

Raman retired from the Indian Institute of Science when he was 60 years old. But he did not retire from the field of science! He founded an institute where he could continue with his research even after retirement. The institute has come to be called the Raman Research Institute. The land for the Institute came as a gift from the then Maharaja of Mysore. For the first year at the Institute, there was no electricity, but that did not deter Raman from carrying out several optical experiments with sunlight, a few lenses and a pair of polaroids.

Several honours were conferred on Raman, including the Bharat Ratna in 1954. In 1924, he was made a Fellow of the Royal Society, London. In 1929, the year before he received the Nobel Prize, he was conferred the knighthood by the British Government. His name now changed to Sir C.V. Raman. Later in life, Raman was simply called Sir C.V. He also won the International Lenin Prize in 1957. When he was offered the Vice-Presidentship of India, Raman asked, "What shall I do with the 'ship'?''

The life of Sir C. V. Raman had been one of unswerving devotion to the pursuit of knowledge, and of unceasing service to the cause of science and the promotion of research in India. When the end came on November 21, 1970, his mortal remains were consigned to the flames in the campus of the

Raman's world of sound, light and colour:
the vibrations of the veena, the whispering gallery of Gol Gumbaj at Bijapur and the tail feathers of the peacock

Institute itself, as per his wishes. No plaque or monument marks the spot — just a solitary tree. Next time you go to Bangalore, visit the Institute, stand before the tree and pay homage to this great son of India.

Raman did some outstanding research on vibrations and sound, and on the theory of musical instruments. He studied how musical instruments like the violin and the veena, could produce harmonious music. Raman's studies on the violin were quite extensive and resulted in a remarkable book. Running to 158 pages, it is entitled, *On the Mechanical Theory of Vibrations of Musical Instruments of the Violin Family,* which is referred to by acousticians even today, 75 years after it was written!

A copy of Raman's monograph on the violin has an inscription by the great violinist, Yehudi Menuhin. It says, "In memory of my visit to the Institute, to an authority on sound, from an ignorant violinist."

Raman had a particular fascination for the mridangam, a South Indian drum, an accompaniment for a Carnatic music recital. He had even worked out the mathematics of its vibrations. One can only marvel at his experimental skill in producing vibration curves of great precision and sharpness much before the condenser microphone was invented. He extended his studies to the 'whispering galleries', where the architectural and acoustic features of several remarkable structures, such as the Gol Gumbaj in Bijapur and the Victoria Memorial in Calcutta, were discussed. Raman became such an authority on the subject of vibrations and the theory of musical instruments, that he was invited to contribute an article to *Handbuch der Physik,* the German Encyclopaedia of Contemporary Physics.

Raman loved trees, flowers and above all, his rose garden. All the best roses that Bangalore nurseries could supply were bought and planted in his garden. He admired them like a child would admire a new toy.

Colour fascinated Raman to no end, and was the subject of many of his studies. He was particularly fond of the magnificent display of the tail feathers of the peacock. Raman also collected diamonds, which he called the 'Prince of Solids'. He was deeply interested in the physical investigation of the diamond. The need for diamonds, in all sizes, shapes and qualities, became so great that Raman began acquiring them by all possible methods, like purchasing, borrowing from shops and wealthy people. He organised them into a museum and would turn the ultraviolet lights on and off a hundred times, enjoying the sight like a child. Raman was convinced that the intensive study of diamonds could be of importance to physics and chemistry.

DO YOU KNOW?

- The first Nobel Prize for Physics was awarded in 1901 to the German doctor-turned-physicist, Wilhelm Roentgen, for his discovery of X-rays, also called Roentgen Rays after their discoverer.

  The discovery of X-rays brought about a revolution in medical diagnosis and treatment. These rays pass through the body and print a shadow picture of the bones on a sensitive plate.

- Marie Curie, the Polish-born physicist, shared the Nobel Prize in Physics in 1903 with her husband Pierre and another French scientist, for their discovery of radioactivity. Marie Curie was awarded a Nobel Prize again in 1911, this time in chemistry, for her work on radium and its compounds. She became the only person ever to have been awarded the Nobel Prize in both physics and chemistry. The discovery of radium by Curie was a turning point in the treatment of cancer.

- The unit of measurement of radioactivity, used by scientists all over the world is called 'curie', after Marie Curie.

- At 25, William Lawrence Bragg, became the youngest recipient of the Nobel Prize. He and his father, William Henry Bragg, shared the Physics Prize in 1915 for the use of X-rays to study crystal structure.

- In 1921, Albert Einstein received The Nobel Prize for a theory in physics that could be understood by just a few people in the world at that time. Besides contributing to theoretical physics, Albert Einstein wrote several books. He is best known for his Theory of Relativity — a theory that completely revolutionized physics and led, through its equation of mass and energy, to the discovery of the atomic bomb. In spite of Einstein's protests that his findings should not be used for anything but scientific experiments, the atomic bomb was made and used in World War II.

  Once, on being asked to explain the Theory of Relativity, Einstein said, "When a man sits with a pretty girl for an hour, it seems like a minute. But let him sit on a hot stove for a minute and it will seem like more than an hour. That is relativity."

- Jagdish Chandra Bose was one of the pioneers of modern science in India. Though more famous as a biologist, he was a great physicist as well. His discovery of radio waves entitles him to be called the inventor of wireless telegraphy.

The 'Maker' of Artificial Genes

Dr. Hargobind Khorana

(Birth: 1922)

Dr. Hargobind Khorana was responsible for producing the first man-made gene in his laboratory in the early seventies. It was a historic invention which made him famous all over the world. Earlier, in 1968, Khorana shared the Nobel Prize in Physiology or Medicine with M.W. Nirenberg and R.W. Holley. Working independently of one another, all three made contributions to the understanding of the genetic code and how it works in the cell.

Hargobind was born in a village in West Punjab, now in Pakistan, in 1922. Of the hundred people in that tiny village, only those of his family were literate. As a child, Hargobind went to the village school where classes were held in the shade of a big tree.

After doing his M.Sc in Chemistry at the University of Punjab in Lahore, Hargobind went abroad on a government scholarship and took his Ph.D in Organic Chemistry from the University of Liverpool in Britain. As he could not get a suitable job on his return to India, he went back to England for further research.

In 1959, Dr. Khorana, while working at the University of British Columbia in Canada, synthesized a chemical called 'coenzyme A', which is essential for certain processes in the human body. A year later, he moved to the University of Wisconsin in the USA, where he took up the task of building a gene of the bacteria *Escherichia coli* that lives in the intestines of human beings and animals. Piece by piece, he and his team built up the 'gene' of the bacteria. In August 1976, this man-made gene was 'inserted' into *Escherichia coli.* It began to work like its natural gene. The achievement no doubt, was hailed by all, but it had taken several years of consistent labour to produce the artificial gene!

The Medal for Physiology or Medicine (reverse side)
[The inscription reads (word for word): Inventions enhance life which is beautified through art]

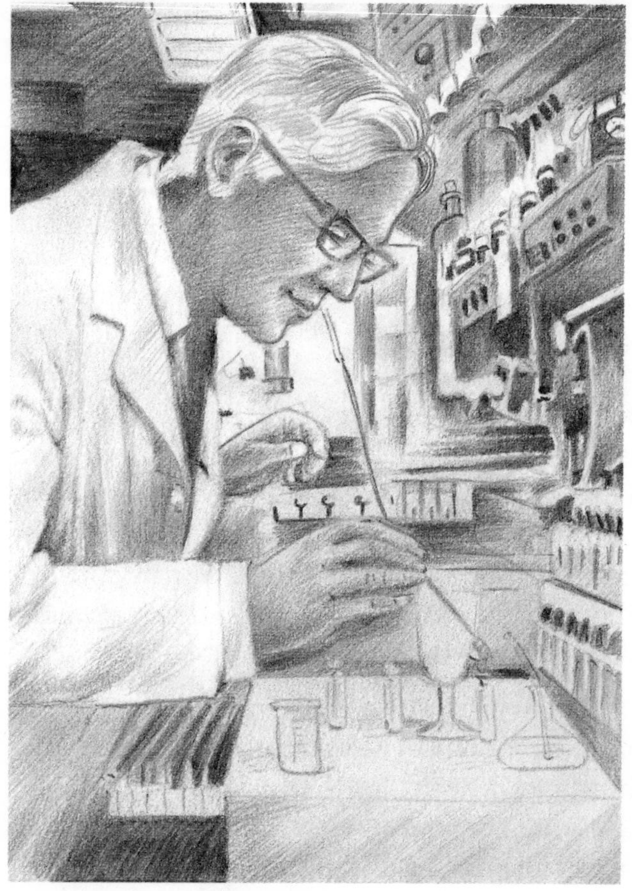

Let us try to understand the mystery of the mechanism of **genes**.

The word 'gene' comes from the Greek word meaning 'to give birth to'. It is a biological unit which passes on 'hereditary' traits or characteristics from one generation to the next. Genes are passed on from parents to their offspring, so children 'inherit' certain traits of their parents. The study and science of 'heredity' is called **genetics**.

The serious studies in genetics started around 1860. Gregor Mendel, an Austrian monk, was the first to perform various experiments on pea plants. He noted that in the seeds from parent plants, there were a large number of different factors that always worked by certain rules. He found that some characteristics occur more often than others and he called them 'dominant' characteristics. The others he called 'recessive'.

It was only 16 years after his death, that other scientists saw how important Mendel's findings were. They called his discoveries **the Mendelian Laws of Inheritance**. Yet, they did not know exactly how the characteristics are passed from parents to offspring.

All living creatures are made up of many cells. The large dense body in the centre of the cell is called the **nucleus**. Each nucleus contains **chromosomes,** thin, thread-like bodies made up of DNA, short for 'deoxyribonucleic acid'. A part of DNA is called gene. Several such genes are present in each chromosome. Thus the chromosome of a cell may contain thousands of genes. The gene transmits characteristics from parents to offspring. A single characteristic is controlled by a pair of genes.

DNA is a mixture of sugar and phosphates carrying the genetic information. A model of DNA looks like a rope, twisted into the form of a ladder. Scientists tried to find out how chemical messages or the sequence of the bases along the DNA molecule control cells, the basic units of life.

The secret of the DNA code of life was finally unravelled by Dr. Khorana who showed how the genetic code determines all life processes by directing the synthesis of all cell proteins.

The unravelling of the genetic code has opened the way to a whole new branch of science called 'Genetic Engineering'. Genetic engineering makes possible the creation of new forms of life by altering the genes in DNA. Plant and animal breeders can now produce organisms with almost any mix of characteristics. In 1997, a team of Scottish scientists produced the first live, healthy sheep clone, named Dolly. It is now possible to cure genetic diseases either by repairing the defective gene or introducing normal functioning genes. This has led to novel diagnostic tools for inherited human diseases, as well as for cancer and AIDS.

DO YOU KNOW ?

- Hippocrates, the Greek physician, is known as the 'father of medicine'. More than two thousand years ago, he wrote the first records of medical observations, and so created a new scientific base for medical practice. The **Hippocrates Oath**, an ethical code formulated by him, is still administered to medical graduates.
- Ayurveda is India's 3000 years old system of medicine. Its name is derived from the Sanskrit *ayur* meaning 'life', and *veda* meaning 'knowledge', that is, 'the knowledge of life.' Ayurveda is second only to homoeopathy in its popularity as an alternate system of medicine.
- Charaka, one of the best known physicians in Indian Ayurvedic medicine, knew the fundamentals of genetics some 2000 years ago. For instance, he knew the factors determining the sex of a child. A genetic defect in a child, like blindness, according to him, was not due to any defect in the mother or the father, but in the ovum or sperm of the parents — an accepted fact today.
- Sushruta is regarded as the 'father of plastic surgery'. He devised an artificial nose more than 2,500 years ago in India. He also performed eye operations for cataract. His techniques were followed by the British surgeons who, in turn, introduced rhinoplasty to the world, as late as the 18th century.
- Homoeopathy, which was developed in Germany in the early 19th century, has over ten lakh practitioners in India today — more than anywhere else in the world. There are about 138 homoeopathic colleges spread all over the country at present. The Calcutta Homoeopathic Medical College and Hospital, founded in 1881, is the oldest and biggest in India.
- Prafulla Chandra Ray is considered the 'father of modern chemistry' in India. He converted the waste cattle bones into a medicinal compound from which a nerve tonic was made in 1896. The Bengal Chemical and Pharmaceutical Works, now one of the biggest chemical firms in the country, was started by him.

An Angel of Mercy

Mother Teresa

(1910 - 1997)

Mother Teresa was God's special gift to mankind. Her life was a story of love and compassion. To millions of the sick, abandoned poor and the dying, she brought help and relief. She dedicated her life to the service of the 'poorest of the poor', as she believed that in serving the poorest, she was serving God.

Mother Teresa was born Agnes Gonxha Bojaxhiu in Skopje, then in Albania, Yugoslavia, on August 27, 1910. As a twelve-year-old, she decided to become a nun, and at 18, she joined the Order of Loreto nuns in Ireland. On joining the order, Agnes took on the name 'Teresa'. There, in that distant land, she would get the call to go to India. "It is a missionary country like the countries of Africa," she explained when asked why she had chosen India. And it was in Calcutta that she arrived in 1929, to become a teacher in a Loreto school. "I love teaching most of all," she said. She devoted 17 years of her life to it.

On September 10, 1946, while on a train journey to Darjeeling, she heard the 'Voice of God' from within, asking her to leave the convent and serve the 'poorest of the poor' of Calcutta. "The message was clear," she said, "but I had to wait for the permission from the Pope to be released from the Loreto Order and to start on my own."

After getting the Pope's permission, she left the school, discarded the black-and-white dress of the Loreto nuns, and wore a coarse, blue-bordered sari. Sister Teresa became an Indian citizen in the year 1948 and came to be known as Mother Teresa. With the Bible in hand, a cross pinned to her shoulder, less than Rs. 5 in hand, and with boundless faith and courage in her heart, she set up her organisation, the Missionaries of Charity. It began formally in October, 1950.

The Medal for Peace (reverse side)
[The inscription reads (word for word): For peace and brotherhood of men]

Feeding the destitute

In the early days, both money and help were scarce. But that did not discourage her from entering a slum, gathering a few children around her, picking up a stick and drawing the letters of the Bengali alphabet on the ground. Soon someone donated a chair, another a blackboard and teachers volunteered their services, and the school became a reality. "If He shows you a need to be served, he will provide the resources," she would say.

The first woman that Mother Teresa picked up from the streets was half eaten by rats and ants. Mother could not get her admitted to a hospital, and the woman breathed her last in Mother's arms. It strengthened her resolve to build a home where the abandoned could live and die with dignity. The search led her to Kalighat where the Calcutta Corporation gave her some empty halls. This became her first home for the dying and she called it **Nirmal Hriday,** 'the Place of the Pure Heart'. "Nobody there has died feeling unwanted or unloved. We help the poor to die in peace with God," she said. From **Nirmal Hriday,** grew 62 Homes for the dying poor all over India. They are run by the Missionaries of Charity.

Mother Teresa's second mission of mercy was towards the poor, orphaned and abandoned children. The **Nirmal Shishu Bhavan** was the first of her many Homes for them. "The poor want your love, not only your service. To give love, you have to give a part of yourself," is the unusual message on a colourful poster for the visitors to the Bhavan. Over the years, about 10,000 children have been brought up at the Shishu Bhavan. As babies they were cradled in the arms of the Sisters, and as they grew up, they were schooled and trained for a profession. Later, they were helped to settle down in life.

The third great focus of her work was for lepers. Victims of leprosy, usually shunned, disowned and abandoned by their families, are forced to beg and steal. Mother understood their despair and set up a shop under a tree in a lepers' colony, and gave out medicines, dressings and dispensed simple treatments. From under the tree, she moved on to a van and then to a mobile clinic. When the authorities donated some land, Mother built **Prem Nivas,** 'the Home of Love'. Now lepers come here from all over India. "When I wash a leper's wounds, I feel I am nursing the Lord Himself," said Mother. 'Touch a leper, touch him with love,' was Mother's motto.

Mother Teresa's first foundation outside India was started in 1965. Gradually, the Missionaries of Charity became a world-wide congregation of thousands of sisters and brothers, priests and volunteers, drawn from various nationalities. Spread over 120 countries, the order runs educational establishments, clinics, homes for the poor and hospices for AIDS patients. When asked about the transition of her Missionaries of Charity from a small Order to a large institution, Mother retorted, "It is **not** an institution. It is love in action. It is the sign that it is God's work, not my work. Although we have grown so big, we are still a family."

A grateful world showed Mother Teresa their respect by giving her numerous awards, at both national and international levels. The Nobel Peace Prize, the Leo Tolstoy International Award, the Bharat Ratna, the British Order of Merit, the Ceres Medal of the FAO — the list is endless. To put it briefly, since the Nobel Peace Prize in 1979, she has received over 50 national and international awards. "These awards are not for me. They are for the poor who are being recognised," she said. She wanted nothing for herself, for she considered herself an instrument of God. All the cash awards were spent on the poor and the suffering. When the former Pope, Paul VI gifted her the magnificent limousine in which he travelled in India, she organised a raffle for the car and the money collected was spent on a leprosy centre. When Mother received the Pope John XXII Peace Prize in 1971, the cash award of $ 21,500 which it carried, went to the cause of leprosy patients. The construction of a Children's Home in Agra would have been abandoned if Mother had not donated the cash prize of Rs. 50,000 which came with the Magsaysay Award.

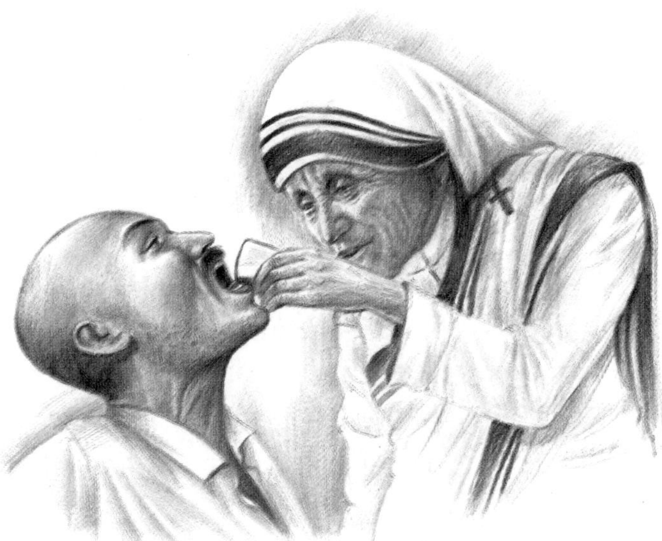

Love and care from Mother

Since the poor are to be found in all parts of the world, Mother travelled wherever she could, setting up islands of hope for the the neglected and the poor. She had once said that she was prepared to go to the Moon, 'if there are poor there'. Through her thoughts, words and deeds, Mother showed the world that if one has the will and the 'milk of human kindness', one can "see God in every human being. If you judge people, you have no time to love them."

Mother Teresa's most favoured word was 'beautiful'. For her, "to do something beautiful for God is what life is all about. Let every action of mine be something beautiful for God," she used to say. Frequently, she would quote the words,

I was hungry and you fed me,
I was naked and you clothed me,
I was sick and you visited me,
I was homeless and you took me in,
Whatever you did, you did it to me.

"O beloved sick," she once prayed, "how doubly dear you are to me, when you personify Christ, and what privilege is mine to tend you."

Listening to the plight of unwed mothers

On one occasion, when Mother had overcome a rather serious health problem, and someone told her how happy everyone was to have her back in good health, she replied with a smile, "Well, I went to heaven's gate and St. Peter told me: 'Why have you come here, there are no poor people in heaven to be cared for!' So I came back to continue my work."

Mother Teresa died on September 5, 1997, in Calcutta. As the world's most recognised symbol of compassion, hundreds of important Indian and world personalities came to pay homage to the 'Saint of the Gutters'. A gentle drizzle fell while the funeral service was being conducted in the Netaji Indoor Stadium, almost as if the weather signified the feelings of the mourners. She was buried in the Mother House, the headquarters of the Order of Missionaries of Charity.

Tributes poured in from all over for one who had dedicated her life to the suffering humanity. The most apt, perhaps, was by the French President Jacques Chirac, "This evening there is less love, less compassion, less light in the world."

Mother Teresa drew her strength from prayer and the Mass that she attended every morning. For her, the Christ on her crucifix and the one who lay abandoned on the streets were not different from each other. Hundreds and thousands of suffering human beings benefited from Mother's love and care. She used to say, "My work is just a drop when what is needed is an ocean of compassion. If I did not put in that one drop, the ocean would be one drop less."

Mother Teresa showed us the path of service — the most beautiful form of worship. Her indomitable faith, love for all, hard work, perseverance and selfless service will continue to inspire the people of the world for years to come.

DO YOU KNOW?

- Jean Henri Dunant, a Swiss businessman, was awarded the first Nobel Peace Prize of 1901 for founding the **Red Cross**.

  The Red Cross is an international organisation concerned with alleviating suffering and promoting public health. It was founded in 1864 on the insistence of Jean Henri Dunant, who had witnessed the slaughter of 30,000 soldiers at the Battle of Solferino during the Franco-Austrian War. He formed a permanent relief society for those wounded in war and called it the International Red Cross. Its symbol, a red cross on a white background, is the reverse of the flag of Switzerland, the birthplace of the society. Today the Red Cross has more than 200 million members in 150 countries, and its work has expanded to help relieve the suffering caused by political upheavals, natural disasters and war.

  The Red Cross is the only institution to have won the Nobel Peace Prize thrice — in 1917, 1944 and 1963 — for its relief work and other humanitarian activities.

- Amnesty International, the worldwide organisation for the defence of human rights, is one of the few institutions to have won the Nobel Peace Prize. Most winners have been individuals. Amnesty was awarded the Peace Prize in 1977 for the organisations's help in paving the way 'for freedom for justice, and thereby also for peace in the world'.

  Amnesty International was founded in 1961 by a British lawyer, Peter Benenson. It has no political ties and campaigns for the release of prisoners of war, fair and prompt trials for political prisoners, and the abolition of torture and capital punishment.

- Florence Nightingale (1820 – 1910), like Mother Teresa, dedicated herself to the selfless service of the sick and the wounded with a missionary zeal. Known throughout the world as 'The Lady with the Lamp' (she used to carry a lamp while visiting patients at night), Florence organised a team of 38 women nurses at the time of the Crimean War. She did such a commendable job that by the end of the war, she had become a legend. She established a nursing school in London and encouraged the British women to join the medical profession.

  She was the first woman to be given the British Order of Merit.

An Economist of the Downtrodden

Professor Amartya Sen

(Birth: 1933)

Professor Amartya Sen, the noted economist-philosopher, became the first Asian economist and the sixth Indian to get the coveted Nobel Prize in Economic Sciences for 1998, instituted by the Bank of Sweden in the memory of Alfred Nobel. The citation of the Royal Swedish Academy, which decides upon the Nobel Prizes, highlights Sen's empirical studies on famines, and draws attention to his 'several key contributions to welfare economics ...'

Sen was born in Santiniketan in 1933. He was named 'Amartya'— 'the one who deserves immortality,' by Rabindranath Tagore who was himself the first to put India on the Nobel Prize map. "I can see the boy will grow into an outstanding person,'' the poet told Amartya's parents.

As a schoolboy in Santiniketan, Sen thought variously of becoming a Sanskrit scholar like his grandfather, a mathematician another time, and a couple of years later, a physicist. But when he entered Calcutta's Presidency College, after topping the intermediate examination, he was in no doubt about his true calling — Economics. Destiny, perhaps, also played a part in this. As a boy of ten, he had witnessed the horrors of the Bengal famine of 1943, a man-made catastrophe in which five million people died. He had seen people dying in front of his house. He recalls, "The streets were full of emaciated looking faces and people were dying in very large numbers. It made me think about what causes famine and when I took on the famine work in a formal way 30 years later, I was still quite haunted by the memories of that period.''

Sen started his career as a Professor of Economics at Jadavpur University. He then shifted to the Delhi School of Economics

The Medal for the Prize in Economic Sciences
(reverse side)

where he taught for eight years. Then, he moved to the London School of Economics before becoming the Drummond Professor of Political Economy at Oxford. Subsequently, he was Professor of Economics and Philosophy for nearly a decade at the Harvard University (USA). He left this prestigious job to take over as Master of Trinity College at Cambridge — a singularly honoured position, as no Indian had ever occupied it till then.

Prof. Sen has always been a good communicator. As a distinguished teacher, he has produced a generation of students and admirers in India and abroad. He is also a prolific writer. He has authored 21 books, apart from nearly 200 research papers and articles. His writings span many areas. In all his works, his fundamental concern has been the well-being of the people, especially the poor. He has analysed the causes of famine and starvation. In one of his famous books *Poverty and Famines — An Essay on Entitlement and Deprivation*, he challenged the popular notion that the shortage of food was the most important cause of famine. He showed that other factors also contributed to it and that a famine could occur even without any significant drop in the supply of food articles. He says that his work was guided by a desire to discover the roots of poverty. "I was always concerned for the economically disadvantaged, the poor, the hungry, the unemployed, the starving. This was always a feature of my work.'' No wonder he has been hailed by *The Wall Street Journal* as a 'Student of the World's Miserable'.

Prof. Sen's work on poverty and famine led to the drawing of the 'poverty line', a measure widely used by the UN and other agencies to determine the level of poverty in a particular country. One of his most dramatic findings relates to the devastating results of the inequality between men and women. This is because of an ancient but unfortunate Indian tradition where males are favoured over females in terms of the 'entitlement' (Sen's term) of food and nourishment.

Prof. Sen believes in 'Welfare Economics' and Social Choice Theory. He emphasises on the need for education for all-round development. Without education, human capabilities are reduced and people are not able to take advantage of economic opportunities.

Prof. Sen has planned to share the prize money with a charity trust to be named 'Pratiti Trust' after his house in Santiniketan. "The trust will focus on education and health care which have been my major concerns over the years,'' Sen said. Describing it as a 'tiny effort', he said that the beneficiaries, to begin with, would be in India and Bangladesh. Sen had spent his childhood in Bangladesh where he studied till class three.

In spite of his long years of living and working abroad, Prof. Sen says, "I value retaining my Indian nationality.'' Despite being deeply attached to the country of his birth, its people, social values and traditions, he has an outlook which is not limited by national boundaries.

In January 1999, Prof. Amartya Sen was awarded the Bharat Ratna, India's highest civilian honour.

DO YOU KNOW ?

- *Arthashastra*, the science of political economy, of the fourth century BC, is considered the oldest treatise on government and economics. It was written by Kautilya, who was also known as 'Chanakya'. *Arthashastra* deals with a vast variety of subjects and covers almost every aspect of the theory and practice of government.
- Economics is generally thought of as the 'Science of Wealth'. The word 'wealth' is derived from the old English word 'weal', which means well-being, happiness, prosperity and welfare. In its larger context, economics deals with the material welfare of mankind, and can be defined as the science of the production, distribution and consumption of wealth.
- In 1776, Adam Smith, a Scottish professor of moral philosophy, published his book entitled *Inquiry into the Nature and Causes of the Wealth of Nations.* A masterpiece, the book exercised a tremendous influence on the development of economic theory in relation to the material affairs of the society. He said that wealth consists not in precious metals but in the goods men use and consume, and produce by their labour. Adam Smith has been called the 'father of modern economics'.
- There are some popular 'theories' or 'laws' in economics, derived by economists. Some of them are:

  The Malthusian Theory: Population has a tendency to multiply faster than the food supply. As a result, famine, disease or war eventually take over. Thomas Malthus was a British economist.

  Sir Thomas Gresham's Law states: Bad money drives out good money, that is, the public tend to hoard coins with greater silver or bullion content. Don't we try to discard old torn notes in favour of new, crisp ones?

  Law of Supply and Demand: An increase in supply tends to lead to a lower price for any particular product, unless there is an increase in demand, and vice versa.

  Parkinson's Law states: Work expands to fill the time available for its completion. Or, that the amount of work done varies inversely to the number of people employed.

FACT FILE

Some eminent scientists, authors and great people did not get the Nobel Prize, although their contributions were very important and significant. They also met the conditions for eligibility (they were living when the prizes were constituted, that is, from 1901 onwards) and were even nominated. Six of them are listed below:

- Thomas Alva Edison (1847–1931) was a giant among inventors. He patented over a thousand inventions in his lifetime, including the phonograph (an early record player), the microphone and an early cine-camera. But his most important invention was the electric bulb.
- Joseph Lister (1827–1912), a medical scientist and surgeon, pioneered antiseptic surgery. Earlier, surgeons carried out operations wearing their ordinary clothes. They did not wear surgical gloves or masks. Even the instruments used were not sterilized to kill germs. By using carbolic acid as an antiseptic, he reduced danger to life from surgery.
- Mark Twain was the pen-name of S.L. Clemens (1835–1910), a prolific American writer. He is best known today for his book *The Adventures of Tom Sawyer.* Written for children, it deals with the adventures of young Tom and his friend in a small town on the banks of the Mississippi River. His other book *The Adventures of Huckleberry Finn,* has become a classic, meant for readers of all ages.
- Albert Sabin (born 1906), a renowned American virologist, developed an oral vaccine (about 1959), to immunise against polio, which is an acute, infectious disease that sometimes kills and sometimes cripples young children. Found throughout the world, cases of paralytic polio occur far more frequently in temperate zones.
- Count Leo Tolstoy (1828–1910), the Russian novelist, achieved fame through his powerful novels like *War and Peace*, *Anna Karenina* and *Resurrection.* He abandoned high society for a simple life of poverty, and devoted himself to village education and famine relief.
- Mohandas Karamchand Gandhi (1869–1948), who was called the **'Mahatma'** (Great Soul), believed that a revolution did not need arms and ammunition. Instead, it needed resistance to oppression. His method, called *satyagraha* (insistence on truth), included all forms of non-violent resistance for achieving political freedom, economic uplift and human equality. There has been universal recognition of his courage, his integrity of purpose, his personal sacrifice and his love for all.